HOME INVE

The First 100 Steps to Home Inventory Professional Success

By Michelle Ketterman, The Inventory Expert

ISBN: 0615594875
ISBN-13:97480615594873

DEDICATION

This book is dedicated to North American Home Inventory Professionals who, like me, struggled and searched to find reputable, dependable, and believable sources of trustworthy professional information and resources but were consistently let down by fake awards, false testimonials, and other ridiculous shenanigans found. The time has come for competent and trustworthy Home Inventory Professionals to stand up, band together, and make a difference in this relatively new industry.

1
INTRODUCTION

The third-party Home Inventory profession is not new. As long as there has been property insurance, there has been a need for third-party home inventory. Although the profession has been around for many years, most Americans had not heard of the service until recently.

Historically, many Home Inventory Professionals (HIPs), have been reluctant to share their knowledge and experience with newcomers to the field. Luckily, the days of "turf protection" and holding information hostage are over. Why? Because today, HIPs from around the country understand that by joining forces and working together to educate consumers and standardize the industry, we will all be more successful. HIPs are realizing that there is power in numbers and by combining efforts; great strides are being made in the area of Home Inventory consumer education.

The greater population is becoming aware of the need for a Home Inventory yet they are still unaware that there are actual professionals experienced and proficient in speedy and accurate documentation. With the refreshing new open lines of communication come a new demand for qualified HIPs. After 15 years as a HIP, I have tried almost everything to attract clients and spread the word about the importance of third-party Home Inventory. I am very pleased to provide this list of the first 100 steps to help new HIPs get started in a fraction of the time it has taken others who came before them.

2
THE HOME INVENTORY PROFESSION

A home inventory is simply a list of items in a home or business with accompanying photographs. The more accurate and comprehensive the Home Inventory reports, the better.

Home Inventory reports have many uses, but the two most common uses are to aid in the thorough completion of insurance claim forms and for stolen property identification reports. Obviously, the more detailed information provided in a home inventory, the more weight the Home Inventory carries. A Home Inventory performed by a qualified third-party HIP holds exponentially more weight than a self-compiled Home Inventory because the reports are compiled by a non-biased third-party.

Notes:

3
YOUR FIRST 100 STEPS

The following ***First 100 Steps to HIP Success*** should help get your new Home Inventory business started. This list is a suggestion meant to help you get started – you may possibly have steps that are not included...so do them too. This list is set up specifically to follow each step in order. The left side pages are intentionally blank to provide space for notes, log in information, phone numbers, web addresses, and so on.

STEP 1

Gather Information. Take your time gathering information about the many challenges, hurdles, and rewards of business ownership from as many different resources and sites as possible. Speak to entrepreneurs in your community and ask them to be frank and candid and share their obstacles and successful tricks to you. DO YOUR RESEARCH!

STEP 2

Start a **journal** of your ideas and include dates and important details. You cannot remember every idea that crosses your mind, but you can rely on your journal during slow times or when you seem to run out of ideas and tactics. Every entrepreneur's well of strategies runs dry from time to time. Having a journal will ensure that you not only have a fresh supply of new approaches to your business, but also that you won't try the same unsuccessful tactics more than once. Your journal will come in handy and could become a powerful tool and resource for your new endeavor as a HIP.

STEP 3

Research industry resources. Look anywhere and everywhere. Make sure you are thorough; do your research and then do more. Find out everything you can about the Home Inventory profession, fellow HIPs, property insurance, and the claims process. Beware of industry forums! There are Home Inventory

Notes:

resources that rely on false positive testimonials for their products. There are also cases of HIP product providers that purposely post unfounded negative reports on their competitor's product. Be smart and don't simply rely on a company's message about themselves, see what others are saying as well.

STEP 4

Read any business and entrepreneurial books, white pages, ebooks, and reports you can find – the more, the better. Don't discount the value of those that have mastered their field; whether related to the Home Inventory profession or not, many valuable insights can be gained from the lessons of others. If you cannot invest in a Kindle, Nook, or iPad, sign up for a free account at Free-EBooks.net and enjoy the many free resources they offer. If there is anyway possible to own a Kindle, I highly recommend it – HIPs can spend a great deal of time traveling to networking and partner meetings, client appointments, and educational events. During time spent driving, the Kindle reads business books out loud, making double use of time driving to appointments. With any eReaders, your entire digital library travels with you making the very best use of your time.

STEP 5

After performing thorough industry research, begin to **define your Home Inventory process**. Your processes will inevitably change with experience, but it is important to begin documenting your processes as you see them initially. There are many things to consider. Will a formal quote be part of your process? Will you offer draft Home Inventory reports allowing clients to edit before finalizing the Home Inventory or will you submit finalized versions without final client input? Visually walk through the Home Inventory process and write questions and process concerns in your journal.

STEP 6

At the beginning of your HIP journey, and **before buying equipment** you may not need, use a basic camera and existing computer. The two main things you will need to begin performing as a HIP are a computer and digital camera.

Notes:

After you have set up your business and have scheduled a couple paying Home Inventories, you can purchase a digital camera best suited to a HIP. I use a Sony CyberShot with 16 mega pixels, 12X optical zoom, with high sensitivity ISO 1250. Unlike other higher priced quality digital cameras, the Sony CyberShot will take crystal clear up-close photos of manufacturer labels, serial numbers, and other small details difficult to capture on standard digital cameras.

STEP 7

Perform your own home inventory. This is probably the **most important** step of becoming a Home Inventory Process. **Never** under estimate the importance of this step. After 15 years of performing countless Home and Business Inventories, the inventory on my own home has been by far the most difficult Home Inventory I have compiled; and I have performed some extreme Home Inventories! By performing your own Home Inventory, you gain the unique perspective of the client and you will soon realize how valuable your time and expertise as a HIP will become. As a Home Inventory client, you will soon understand how difficult it is to stay focused and on task, and how easy distractions present themselves. Distractions like memories attached to items, the desire to make things perfect before the Home Inventory, putting things in their proper place, and so on. Performing your own Home Inventory is a difficult and time-consuming task; there is a reason so few home and business owners are able to compile their own inventories. By being able to relate your experience performing your personal Home Inventory, you will also be prepared to keep your future HIP clients on task and not easily distracted. Many times, sharing my personal Home Inventory experience has served as a catalyst for gaining new clients.

STEP 8

Make a physical folder to store miscellaneous items you come across that can be used in future blog entries. This includes any headlines related to fire, robbery, flood, insurance claims, estate planning, divorce, and so on. Although it is easier and much more green-friendly to save these items electronically, storing them in a single place seems to work better – you can also write notes directly like date of blog, contact history, research, related information, etc.

Notes:

Working with this folder also keeps you in the Home inventory frame of mind and the longer you have this file, the more pertinent information you will find.

STEP 9

Set a work schedule. As an entrepreneur, it is important to set a daily work schedule. Especially as a work-from-home entrepreneur, you will not always be able to adhere to the schedule, but you must have a general idea and plan of hours you intend to work. Without a schedule, it is far too easy to lose track of time and become so engrossed in meetings, research, training, set-up, social media, and countless other things that will begin to monopolize your days. By setting a schedule, you are treating your budding Home Inventory service like an actual business.

STEP 10

Begin **tracking your expenses**. From the very beginning of your Home Inventory adventure, you will incur small expenses and mileage. Even small expenses like batteries for your digital camera, paper, ink, and binders add up. At the beginning of your Home Inventory experience, tracking expenses may seem unnecessary but taking the time to set up practices and procedures now will enable smooth bookkeeping when money and clients begin to steadily flow your way. You will probably never regret remaining budget conscious throughout the set-up process. Zoho.com offers an excellent free on-line accounting resource where you can track expenses, revenue, projections, and create invoices and other reports.

STEP 11

Remember to keep track of all of your **lessons, challenges, and successes**. Inevitably, you will experience many pitfalls and even more triumphs! Use your journal to track each one. Diligently recording these events will help you for years to come. Faithfully using your journal to document your Home Inventory businesses events creates a historical document and helps you track your progress on your journey to Home Inventory success.

Notes:

STEP 12

Organize. Keep your thoughts, to-do lists, and jobs well organized. There are many things for a new HIP to do and plan. Business set-up, process definitions, procedural clarification, meetings, and research are just a few of the countless trivial tasks that must be regularly addressed. With so much to do in only 24 hours each day, successful organization is the only way to ensure the most is accomplished is in least time. Continuously search for better and more efficient ways to remain organized.

STEP 13

Define at least **20 professional goals** you want your business to reach. Set 3 month, 6 month, 1 year, 5 year, and 10-year goals. Spread the goals over a period of time so you have a very clear vision of where you expect to accomplish. Add the goals to your planner/calendar and review them regularly. Goals are not to be set and then forgotten; your goals should be very specific. Instead of setting the goal: *be successful*, set this goal: *earn $_________ by date*, or *complete* _____ *paying home inventories by date*, or *earn enough revenue to hire* ____ *HIPs to work for my Home Inventory service by* ______, etc.

STEP 14

Get an **Accountability Partner.** Accountability Partners meet weekly for nine to twelve months (but never more than a year). Working together, your Accountability Partner and you set goals, plan creative strategies and unique approaches, and most importantly assigns tasks and work with specific deadlines. Small business owners easily get caught up (and sometimes lost) in the large amounts of tasks and research demanded. Accountability Partners push each other. They should not be a spouse, friend, family member, or business partner - it should be a successful businessperson within your community. Ideally, your accountability partner will be someone in a different field and stage in life. There must be absolute confidentiality and trust in each other. If chosen wisely, and Accountability Partner will stretch you and foster an environment of tremendous professional growth. Some of my previous Accountability Partners include a bank Vice President, a marketing genius, an

Notes:

attorney, a graphic designer, and the owner of a $1Mil + construction company. As evident by my former Accountability Partners, they had nothing to do with Home Inventory; not even peripherally. The nature of Accountability Partnerships creates closeness and trust that lasts for years and you will be able to count on them for a long time to come.

STEP 15

Set up your **home office** with **locking cabinets**. Ensure every possible security measurement is taken to protect information and documents. As you perform and compile client Home Inventory, you must securely store confidential and sensitive client information. You need a place used exclusively for your Home Inventory business. If you share a computer with someone else (highly not recommended), have a secure and separate log on exclusively for you work. This book assumes you do not have access to an off site office, but regardless of your location, whether at your home or offsite, no one should have access to this information for any reason; not your spouse, children, friends...NO ONE.

STEP 16

Speak with a **legal professional** about your new Home Inventory business. You need to understand everything legally expected of you as a business owner and as a professional whose job duties include entering home and businesses and collecting and compiling data about their possessions and property. Advice received by legal council is money well spent and should not be overlooked. Fully explain your business and services, not only can they offer great insight, attorneys tend to be excellent referral partners sending clients your way.

STEP 17

Speak with a **CPA** or experienced **business Accountant**. You must continuously remain educated and informed about your financial responsibilities as a business owner. Financial professionals typically share a wealth of knowledge and will most likely provide tons of information and tips for you. Be ready to take plenty of notes and probably get a couple homework assignments too. Again, fully explain your business and services, not only can

Notes:

they offer great insight, CPAs tend to be excellent referral partners sending clients your way. A CPA will explain your various tax responsibilities including:

- Federal Taxes
- State Taxes
- Employment Taxes
- Business Taxes

STEP 18

After speaking with a CPA and attorney, you are ready to choose your Home Inventory business set-up and submit the necessary paperwork to the appropriate city, state, and Federal agencies. The various business set-ups include:

Sole Proprietorship - a single individual operates a business and owns all assets. Typically, when operating a business under a name other than the sole proprietor.

General Partnership - two or more individuals or businesses join to operate a business. A separate business entity exists, but creditors can still look to the partners' personal assets for satisfaction of debts. General partners share equally in assets and liabilities.

Limited Partnership - partnership formed by two or more persons or entities, having one or more general partners and one or more limited partners. General partners share equally in debts and assets, while limited partners have limited debt obligations.

Registered Limited Liability Partnership (LLP) - general partnership that has been registered with the Secretary of State. A partner is not individually liable, under some circumstances, for debts and obligations of the partnership arising from errors, omissions, negligence, incompetence, or malfeasance committed in the course of business by others in the partnership.

Corporation (Corp) - (Subchapter C or S) - two or more individuals, partnerships, or other entities join together to form a separate entity for the purpose of operating a business. A corporation has its own legal identity,

Notes:

separate from its owners. The corporation offers protection to the business owners' personal assets from debts and liabilities relating to the corporation.

Limited Liability Company (LLC) - an unincorporated business entity that shares some of the aspects of Subchapter S Corporations and limited partnerships, yet has more flexibility than traditional business entities.

STEP 19

Create a business **budget** and outline all expenses and timeframes. Be realistic - chances are that your Home Inventory business will not immediately make a profit. Creating well-defined financial projections and expectations provides a means to measure your success and setbacks while allowing you to plan future attacks and campaigns. Do not set unrealistic goals, as they will cause you to doubt your actions, and plans. Include foreseeable equipment purchase and include a line item for miscellaneous expenses of $500 to $1,500.

STEP 20

Choose a **strategic business name**. Remember that third-party Home Inventory is a relatively new Profession and not widely known. Use a self-explanatory name; you do not have the luxury of choosing a mysterious business name or something abstract like your initials until you have established yourself and your reputation.

For example, my original business name was **Asset Inventory Group**. When I would introduce myself, the same reaction was received every time, "If I had assets, I would have you inventory them, but I really don't."

After well over a year of hearing almost the same thing from well over 95% of those I met, I changed my business name to **Home Inventory Experts** and was astounded in the immediate change in reception I received. It literally was the difference between night and day and clients seems to come out of the woodwork, and even better, they sought me out without solicitation!

Several years later after I was well established as THE Home Inventory Expert in the DFW area, I began receiving inquiries as to whether I also performed

Notes:

business inventories, which of course I did. Since I had developed a solid reputation and successfully kept the concept of third-party inventory in the front of business owners and community leader's minds, I changed my business name to **The Inventory Experts** and was very pleased with the results.

I share this story because it is a lesson to remember. As HIPs, it is easy to lose sight of the fact that many people have yet to learn about third-party Home Inventory and we must take every opportunity to explain what we do – starting with our name. Choosing a smart business name could mean the difference between your first Home Inventory client in six weeks instead of six months.

STEP 21

Write your business **Mission Statement**. Write a few sentences that clearly and concisely define the mission of your Home Inventory business. The main goal is to answer this: why does my business exist? What do you stand for? What is important to you? Your Mission Statement should be easy to understand, communicate, and memorize. Include this on your website and marketing materials. Over time, your mission statement may or may not change depending on how your business and market change.

For example, "To provide comprehensive documentation of client property and possessions to ensure the highest insurance claim reimbursement check in the shortest time possible."

STEP 22

Write your business **Vision Statement**. Write a few brief sentences stating exactly what you want your Home Inventory business to accomplish in the next five years. Start by completing this statement: *Five years from now, my Home Inventory business will* ____________________ *by* ____________________________, and see what you come up with.
For example, "We will increase the awareness of our company along with the importance of third-party home inventory by strategically marketing our services, exceeding client expectations, and using excellence as our measuring stick."

Notes:

STEP 23

Write your **Values Statement**. Choose 5 words or 1-2 phrases that define the core values of your Home Inventory business. Focus on guiding principles and positive statements and make them brief.
For example, "As a company, we value confidentiality, integrity, respect, and ethical practices. We are committed to our maintaining the security of client data and pride ourselves on protecting it by every measure at our disposal. We hold ourselves accountable to our clients by providing results, security, and the highest quality in everything we do."

STEP 24

Prepare a current **Business Plan** for your Home Inventory business. **DO NOT SKIP THIS STEP!** There are many useful and free tips and templates at sba.gov.

A solid business plan should include:

Executive Statement – this is usually at the beginning of a business plan, but completed last. This section should give a thorough overview and provide a complete picture of your business.

Mission Statement - make sure this section reflects your reasons for being in business.

Describe Your Business and include all aspects in complete detail. Include what makes your business unique.
Include short and long goals including income, client, and educational goals.

Potential Customers – including who buys your product, who needs your services, what they look for, and why they need you.

Competition Analysis because you cannot know your chances for success if you do not know what you are facing in the way of competition. As a HIP, our biggest competition is usually lack of consumer knowledge.

Notes:

Financial Analysis is important because you need to take a realistic look at your finances. Include all the money you pay out each month for personal and expected business expenses, versus how much you realistically expect to earn each month. Remember to list everything.

Marketing is where you list all the places you will advertise or market your business. Don't overlook anything. You can drum up a lot of business by giving a free presentation at a local homeowner's association meeting, Chamber of Commerce, or community event

STEP 25

Determine how you will **fund your Home Inventory** venture until it becomes profitable. Although relatively inexpensive to start a Home Inventory service, there will still be expenditures. Be specific about funding sources. For example, will you continue to work a part time job until clients become steady? Is your family in a position to rely on one income until you establish yourself? It is always easier to move forward with a plan, so do not neglect to thoroughly plan your finances with everyone on the same page. This is a critical step and predetermined financial plans are always useful.

STEP 26

Choose a **business mailing address**. Even in the age of the internet, consumers still expect a local mailing address; they want to know where you hang your hat. Considering the weight and seriousness of what HIPs do, and it is important that you establish your presence in an area. With Google business directory and maps, a photo will often appear next to your business listing. For many obvious reasons, you do not want your home address appearing everywhere you market yourself. A post office box usually costs less than $100 per year. A box at a local UPS Store and similar shops usually costs less than $150 per year and gives your business a physical street address.

STEP 27

Now that you have decided your legal business set-up, submit an **Assumed Name Certificate** to your Secretary of State office. A fictitious name (or

Notes:

assumed name, trade name or DBA name, which is short for "doing business as") is a business name that is different from your personal name, the names of your partners or the officially registered name of your LLC or corporation and must be registered in your state. In most states, it costs less than $20 to submit an Assumed Name Certificate.

STEP 28

After receiving your Assumed Name Certificate, **register** your business with state and county offices.

STEP 29

Obtain all necessary **business licenses and permits** - remember: there is NO Home Inventory Professional's license in ANY state. Do not try to purchase a Home Inventory Professional's license and do not advertise that you have one.

STEP 30

Banks will not allow you to open a business account without an official Assumed Name Certificate. Now that you have yours, open a **checking account** for your Home Inventory business.

STEP 31

Now that you have a business bank account, rent a **bank safe deposit** box to store customer back ups and important legal documents. Most safe deposit boxes can be rented for $100 or less for a year.

STEP 32

Get **business insurance**. Like banks, most insurance carriers require an Assumed Name Certificate to issue professional liability insurance.

Notes:

Considering the nature of what HIPs do, it is imperative to have professional insurance. I recommend $1MIL/$2MIL, this means I have $1MIL per occurrence with a cap at $2MIL per year.

STEP 33

Create an organized method for **saving business receipts**. As you open bank accounts, get business insurance, rent safety deposit and mail boxes, make sure to keep all receipts in a neat, organized system.

STEP 34

Whether you think you will need them or not, log all **business miles**. This is as easy as keeping a spiral bound notebook in your vehicle. Be sure to include the date, beginning and ending mileage, and reason for travel.

STEP 35

Design and organize a CRM (Customer Relation Management) tool to keep track of all contacts, clients, strategic partners, etc. This may seem a bit over the top at this point, but if you set these systems in place when you are just starting and have little or no clients, when the clients come, your processes will be in place and you will be ready to handle your new clients and workload flawlessly. Zoho.com provides a great, free on-line resource.

STEP 36

Set up an accounting **record keeping system** such as QuickBooks, Quicken, or a free on-line product like zoho.com. Most accounting packages allow direct bank statement downloads. This saves an enormous amount of time for small business owners.

Notes:

STEP 37

Create a QR Code linked to your phone number to use on business cards and marketing materials. Initially used for tracking inventory parts in vehicle manufacturing, a QR Code is a two-dimensional barcode, which has encoded in it a URL, text, or other information. Most smart phones have QR reading apps and QR scanners. Since the QR codes originated as part of inventory control, as Home Inventory Professionals, it is recommended to incorporate QR codes into your marketing materials.

STEP 38

By now, you have spent a good deal of time researching the Home Inventory profession and working on your Home Inventory service branding and identity. It's now time to design your Home Inventory Business **logo**.

STEP 39

Create a **style guide**. A style guide is a piece of paper with font names, sizes, and their color along with logo color schemes and any images used in the marketing and promotional pieces for your Home Inventory service. This seems like a trivial step, but taking a few moments to list these seemingly unimportant details will go a long way toward presenting the consistent and professional image your Home Inventory service deserves. Not to mention that a style guide saves a great deal of time because it eliminates guesswork and redesigning.

STEP 40

Create your **company tag line**. A tag line is a memorable, competitive, and self-explanatory phrase that describes your company, services, or target client. Generally, taglines are used for quite a while and help build brand identity. As a HIP, make the absolute most of your tag line.

I received much praise and chuckles from this easily recognizable slogan: "Get the <u>proof</u> of what's under your <u>roof</u>...because your pictures could be worth a

Notes:

thousand bucks." This tag line made me memorable and relatable and I believe directly resulted in many sales.

STEP 41

Create an introductory **company slogan**. Unlike a tag line, a slogan is used for specific campaigns, promotions, or products. If you find yourself stuck and needing fresh slogan ideas, start at sloganizer.com. Sloganizer is an elementary free on-line tool that automatically generates slogan ideas.

STEP 42

Design and order your **business card** and include your business name, slogan, tagline, logo, and QR code that leads to your website. Use and update your style guide as appropriate. VistaPrint.com and GotPrint.com are great resources for very inexpensive, and sometimes free business cards.

STEP 43

Join Toastmasters. Regardless of your speaking experience or anxiety level, join Toastmasters. Period. If you have 10 years experience speaking publicly, you still have room to improve, and HIPs need to be as polished as possible. Let's face it, many experienced speakers are not nearly as good as they think they are and are often sloppy and less articulate than they realize.

STEP 44

Create your 30-60 second **elevator speech**. The concept of an elevator speech is you have to convey your message succinctly in the amount of time it would take to ride an elevator. This is an introduction to you and your Home Inventory business. Always mention why someone would hire you to perform a third party Home Inventory. A catchy slogan or tagline is a great way to wrap up an elevator speech.

Notes:

STEP 45

Tell Everyone! Every interaction is an opportunity to share what you do and why. Many people still haven't heard of Home Inventory. Educate and inform and clients **will** find you! Be proactive and speak to everyone; when you are standing in line, at the gas pumps, getting a hair cut, shopping at the mall, picking up dry cleaning, and so on.

STEP 46

Once you have a business name, logo, professional insurance and bonding and you have chosen on your image and branding, join **The Inventory Institute** and take advantage of the backlinks, press releases, promotions, and education. Studies have shown that companies that actively participate in true industry associations (not those affiliated with particular products) are stronger than those that don't.

STEP 47

Keep a **list of all questions** asked by everyone you talk to about Home Inventory. You will be surprised how often you are asked the same questions. These questions and especially their answers are great resources for promotional materials. When you know what people are curious about relating to Home Inventory, you can address it.

STEP 48

Clearly **define your niche**. Define what type of Inventories you plan to specialize in? Home or Business? Standard or specialized? Begin to develop a **Marketing Plan** by creating a realistic list of actions with solid and strategic action steps along with reachable deadlines.

Notes:

STEP 49

Order polo or dress shirts with your Home Inventory company logo embroidered on them. These items are not as expensive as they used to be, and they go a very long way towards helping you look professional and legitimate. To save money at the beginning of your Home Inventory adventure, only purchase one or two shirts – you can always buy more later. Luckily, my shirts were embroidered with my signature logo shield and no words. This came in very handy when I changed my business name. Since I did not change the graphic, I have been able to use the same shirts for many years. Avoid using a screen printer with mandatory minimum pieces per order. If you cannot find a local provider who does not require minimums, use MrsGsTees.com. They are based in the DFW area and not only will they make 'one or a ton,' their work and customer service is second to none. I wanted something more than polo shirts, and Mrs. G was able to find top quality silk shirts to embroider. (See my headshot at the end of this book for an example.)

STEP 50

Get a **professional head shot**. If you cannot afford one, try bartering with a professional photographer. If you cannot find a barter-friendly photographer, have a friend take a few head shots, but make it a priority to have a professional head shot as soon as possible. Choose one headshot that looks most professional; your goal is not to look cute or trendy. You want to look traditional, confident, serious, and secure. The chosen headshot will be used on your website, all promotional material, your email signature block, and all social media profiles. Consistency is the name of the game when it comes to headshots. Regarding social media: do not change your profile picture more than once a year. Purposely repeating so you remember: consistency is the name of the game where headshots are concerned!

STEP 51

Purchase a URL and **create a website**. Your URL does not need to be your business name. Every business needs a website, even if only a one page Word Press site or Facebook fan page. Be creative with your URL. With the popularity of QR codes and automatic links, website names are not as

Notes:

important as they once were. On the other hand, your URL could be used as another way to communicate your message or your product. For example, my URL is www.ProveItsYours.com. There are countless creative URLs still available. For unique word combination possibilities, play with the Google Wonder Wheel (a keyword phrase finder) and look for URLs that use lots of key words!

STEP 52

Sign up for **Linked In**, use your new headshot and complete your profile 100%. Link to every professional you know. Many professionals and decision makers judge your relevance and trustworthiness based on your number of Linked In connections. Request recommendations and endorsements. Join groups – Home Inventory groups and strategic partner groups like local insurance or realtor groups to name a few. Do NOT register for Linked In only to complete your profile and expect business to come your way. You must actively participate in Linked In. **Never** assume that on-line relationships do not require the same attention that face-to-face relationships demand. Remember, these are real people on the other end of their profile the same as you and should be treated as such.

STEP 53

Create a blog. A blog is very important because it gives the readers a real sense of who you are and what you and your Home Inventory service stand for. It has been said that a website is like a dining room – rarely used with everything in its place and in perfect condition; and a blog is like the kitchen – used often (if not daily), sometimes people stop by and visit, and sometimes you make a mess that needs to be cleaned up. Whether you blog daily or monthly, always be consistent. If you do not have the know-how or desire to house a blog on your main website, many free blogging sites are available such as blogspot.com and blogger.com.

Notes:

STEP 54

Create your Home Inventory **Facebook fan page**. Facebook terms do not allow selling on personal pages so start a fan page immediately. Ask Home Inventory peers and other friends to 'like' your page. Once your page has 25 fans, get a vanity URL at facebook.com/username. A Facebook vanity URL changes: http://www.Facebook.com/yourname/random#s to: http://www.Facebook.com/PageName.

Create a custom graphic or use your headshot or logo as the profile picture. As with all social media sites, do not change your profile photo too often – be consistent with your branding.

STEP 55

Create a **Twitter.com account**, use your new headshot, and complete 100% of your profile. A great Twitter resource is Jeff Goin's blog. One of my favorite posts is below. Jeff's blog URL is http://goinswriter.com. I recommend anyone interested in keeping up with the latest Twitter news follow his blog.

TWITTER MANNERS 101

1. Be gracious.
2. Be social. Twitter is about conversation, not monologue.
3. Say "thank you" (a lot).
4. Use the @ reply to publicly thank someone.
5. Don't just follow people; *engage* them.
6. Have a sense of humor.
7. Refrain from flaming Use your words to encourage and lift up rather than to tear down. Never underestimate the power of a tweet.
8. Don't follow someone expecting him to follow you back. Follow because you're interested in what the person has to say. (Conversely, and somewhat ironically, if someone does follow you, it's courteous to follow back.)
9. Be informal. Have fun. Don't treat it as a chore.
10. Don't hound influential people, begging them to read your blog or retweet you. Win their trust and influence by being remarkable and serving them *first*. My best strategy for networking is serving others.

Notes:

11. Hold back the urge to tweet too much (more than 20 times per day). If you have a lot of ideas, use a program like Hootsuite or Cotweet to schedule your tweets so that they can be spaced out.
12. Listen to your followers.
13. Show interest in others, before asking them to care about you (or what you do).
14. Ask questions.
15. Don't be afraid to ask for a retweet when it's really important. (This is best utilized when it's to help out someone else.)
16. Tell the truth.
17. Don't tweet in the third person (Jeff hates it when you do that — it's so Facebook circa 2008).
18. Don't retweet people who retweet you, unless you're responding and quoting them. e.g. "RT @JeffGoins are you crazy?! // You bet."
19. Promote other people's stuff (blog posts, photos, websites, etc.)
20. Talk about other people more than you do about yourself. A good rule of thumb is the 20:1 ratio.

STEP 56

Create a **Twellow.com account** and register your Home Inventory business in 'the yellow pages for Twitter.' Use your new headshot and complete your profile 100%. Search the Twellow directory for users in your area, strategic partners, or other Home Inventory peers. Twellow is a great tool for Twitter users because its search engines give users more access to other Twitter users than ever before.

STEP 57

Create a **SocialOomph.com account**, use your new headshot, complete your profile 100%, and vet your followers to automatically follow Twitter users that follow you. This is the only time you will most likely sign on to your SocialOomph account.

Notes:

STEP 58

Create a **Meetup.com account**, use your new headshot, complete your profile 100%, and begin looking for networking meetings in your area. Think of anyone that needs your Home Inventory services and then search meetings for them – go where your ideal clients or referral partners go. Always RSVP on line to any meetings you plan to attend. Many times, the number of RSVPs helps attendees decide if they will attend.

STEP 59

Register your Home Inventory business with **Google Places and Google Maps**. Upload your logo, your headshot, and complete your company profile 100% including bios, photos, hours of operation, and reviews. Google Places reviews are a marketing gem because Google lists businesses alphabetically and by reviews, don't overlook this powerful and free marketing tool! Google also ranks businesses based on length of registration with Google. As a new business owner and HIP, the sooner you register your business with Google Places and Maps the better. Along with the number and quality of reviews your business receives on Google Places, the higher you will be ranked in Google Places – this means that if other HIPs come to your area, you will most likely remain the top ranked.

STEP 60

Research **local business journals**. These are usually associated with your local newspaper. Typically, local businesses can register on the business directory for free. Registered users can often list events for free: this includes speaking or seminars about the importance of keeping a current Home Inventory. If nothing else, this is one more place to have a back link to your website. Back links from popular sites help increase your SEO and your visibility, which translates into better on-line presence and reputation for your business.

Notes:

STEP 61

Subscribe to **Google Alerts** to have daily or weekly emails delivered to you with news articles, blog entries, and website content related to subjects of your choice. Popular Google Reader subjects for HIPs include Tornado, Fire, Home Inventory, Flood, Robbery, etc. Fantastic and relevant blog material can be found by using Google Reader and Alerts.

STEP 62

Create a one-page **Press Pack** outlining your professional history, why you are qualified to perform third party Home Inventories, and what sets you apart from others. Include your headshot and all contact information. Your Press Pack (also called a "one-sheeter" or a bio) is used on your website and also sent to media outlets to summarize you and your business.

STEP 63

Order **free publications from FEMA.org**. FEMA happily sends printed publications on all forms of natural and man-made disasters; do not underestimate the power of this free service. Although the FEMA website states maximums of 10 or 15 for each item, they will send up to 250 of each item, but make sure to specify how many of each item you are requesting. If ordering high quantities, add the following statement to the order form:
"Please see the attached order form for FEMA publications. It is a rather large order. These publications will be distributed at large community events as part of a Home Inventory and Preparedness Awareness campaign."

STEP 64

Research various **inexpensive give-aways** related to property ownership, safety, or protection. VistaPrint.com offers many free personalized giveaways where you only pay for shipping. Rack cards, business cards, postcards, note pads, baseball caps, pens, calendars, and magnets are a few of the items that can be ordered from VistaPrint.com.

Notes:

STEP 65

Since you are telling everyone about your business and the importance of Home Inventory, always be ready to convey important points. Carry a business card sized paper with 5 **important facts** and critical points with you at all times. Make sure to keep these important details within arms reach at all times. This seems trivial and often silly, but we often only have one chance to communicate important details...so make it count! Nothing is worse than finally receiving the call from a potential client or referral partner only to forget to mention important details.

STEP 66

With your headshot, one-sheeter, and important facts card in hand, contact local **newspapers and news stations**. Announce your new business and discuss the importance of third-party Home Inventory. Don't be afraid to directly ask what it takes to get some press like an article, editorial, or news spot. Some newspapers appreciate receiving a ready-made article.

STEP 67

Sign up for a free **Press Release** account at www.PRLog.com. Complete your profile 100% and include your headshot and logo. Begin to compile effective keywords and topics for press releases.

STEP 68

Submit your first press release introducing your new company to the world. Include a maximum of four paragraphs and keep it brief. Remember to include some benefits of third party Home Inventory along with your qualifications and contact information. Do not expect overnight success with your press release. It's a numbers game with press releases and the more you submit, the higher your chances of receiving press.

Notes:

STEP 69

Refine Your Processes. Refine, refine, and again refine your processes. Now that you have been setting up your new Home Inventory business hands-on, you have no doubt considered, planned, and mentally reviewed your processes. It is now time to begin documenting your processes and putting them to paper. This will be an on-going process for quite a while but it is important to begin the documentation process. This is the time you will transition from the general business set-up to actually working on the Home Inventory side of things.

STEP 70

Define your **data base fields** including rooms, categories, and conditions. You have already performed your Home Inventory, and given yourself time to let that experience 'marinate.' Compile your initial lists of items in each field. Beginning to work with the Home Inventory database field puts you in the correct Home Inventory mindset and helps get you ready for the next steps. There are many database options for today's HIP. You can design a unique database with Micro Soft Access or another similar program or purchase a pre-made HIP program. A word of caution, do very thorough and diligent research before purchasing any HIP software.

STEP 71

Design Home Inventory reports and includes all data fields. This is as simple as sketching a few ideas on a piece of paper. The important thing is that you thoroughly think through how you want to present the Home Inventory data to your clients. Do **not** give clients Home Inventory reports in a spreadsheet or spreadsheet format. Clients expect professional reports, so set yourself apart from mere Home Inventory 'Providers' and provide professional, attractive, comprehensive, and user-friendly reports – not just spreadsheets.

STEP 72

Determine **pricing structures and packages**. This is one of the toughest exercises so far because you don't know where to begin. Home Inventory is a

Notes:

relatively unknown field and our job as HIPs is to not only set our price, but to also establish the value. Over the past fifteen years, my Home Inventory service has offered pricing for up to 3,000 square feet for $175. We have also charged from 5¢ per square foot to $1 per square foot; and everything in between. For my market, 50¢ per square foot is perfect. One of the biggest mistakes HIPs from around the country make is to charge too little. I often see HIPs offering a full Home Inventory package for $150! If you consider that an experienced HIP can perform a standard Home Inventory in approximately 10 hours, the HIP would only earn $15 per hour BEFORE paying for ink, paper, CDs, gas, etc. This is not smart business. Without realizing it, the HIP is doing himself a great disservice. By valuing his product at such a low price, the HIP is telling potential clients that a third-party Home Inventory is worth less than $15 per hour; this explains the lack of clients. Don't make that same mistake – value your product wisely and set your prices accordingly. If you are not sure how to set your prices, start at a minimum of 35¢ square foot and offer an introductory special of 20¢ per square foot (make sure you mention the discount from your normal price).

STEP 73

If you remember, you performed you own Home Inventory in step #7. It's now time to perform a **practice Home Inventory**. Perform your practice Home Inventory in a friend or family member's home. Make sure they understand that you will be in their home for several hours. Practice your entire process and act as though this is a paying project. Create an invoice that outlines the entire project. Create an invoice for the project; since you most likely performed this project at no cost, include a line item for a discount that zeroes the amount due. Take plenty of notes and ask lots of questions about your processes and how they could be improved. You want as much client feedback as possible. Afterward, fully consider client feedback and how you can improve your processes and flow.

STEP 74

Now that you have performed your own Home Inventory along with a practice Home Inventory, begin to **compile a Sample Home Inventory**. Your Sample Home Inventory serves as a visual example of what your clients should expect.

Notes:

Do **not** cut corners on your Sample Home Inventory – it should be the highest quality example of your work. A Sample Home Inventory is a very powerful tool in the HIP's arsenal so take your time and do it right. Use 28 lb paper and set your printer to the highest print quality. If you 3 ring binders, don't use the cheapest you can find. I use a blue leather view binder ($10 each) and a blue leather portfolio pouch ($15 each) and non-standard dividers ($8 per set). Using these high-price items is one more way to provide professional and top-notch products. This sets you apart from the casual non-professional.

STEP 75

Create the equipment and process **checklist** you will use when packing your Home Inventory Bag before performing a Home Inventory. Include every piece of equipment, batteries, chargers, and cords. Your bag should also include a ruler, tape measure, pens, and anything you can possibly think that you may use. It is always better to be over prepared than underprepared when on-site for a Home Inventory project.

STEP 76

After compiling your personal Home Inventory, a practice Home Inventory, and a sample Home Inventory, it is time to **review your pricing structure**. You have gone through the entire Home Inventory process as a client and also as a HIP. You have also compiled reports and are in the perfect position to review your pricing process. As a HIP, did you feel your current charge was adequate for the time and amount of work you performed? As a client, did you feel your current price was fair for the end result? Consider all angles and points of view. Remember that many people are not familiar with third-party Home Inventory so do not expect to receive educated and sound advice from others. This is not meant to discourage feedback, but many experienced and well-respected business owners said that I would never find anyone willing to pay any amount of money for a Home Inventory. This is because they did not understand the concept of what a HIP provides, so remember all outside opinions you solicit may not be in a position to offer sound advice.

Notes:

STEP 77

Finalize prices and **Home Inventory packages**. Now that you have performed a couple Home Inventories, it is time to define your packages. Create several inventory packages and service products unique to your location and target market. A few package ideas include:
Collector's Inventory - varies greatly based on the project. A collection could be any number of things each changing greatly with each client and project. It is impossible to calculate a Collector's Inventory project without reviewing the collection. Before quoting the project, remember to take a few things into consideration like:

Will the collection need to be unpacked, inventoried, and repacked?

Will the collection be on-site or off?

Does the collection have indentifying marks? Are they individually numbered, signed, etc?

Executive's Inventory - Designed for the business executive with extensive and expensive apparel and accessories. This inventory lists all suits, purses, belts, etc. with extensive cross-referenced photos.

Sportsman's Inventory - Designed for the sports enthusiast with plenty of sports gear and individually lists sports along with plenty of cross-referenced photos.
Workshop Inventory - designed for the Do It Yourselfer with an extensive tool collection; both hand and electric and individually lists tools and equipment and specifies item age, value, and description along with plenty of cross-referenced photos.

Jewelry Inventory - individually lists jewelry including high-ticket items along with costume jewelry and common baubles.

STEP 78

Design and create your **quote sheet** and include all of your inventory packages and pricing. Include all disclaimers, an expiration date, and contact

Notes:

information. Find quote sheet templates on Google Documents and Microsoft and OpenOffice templates to name a few. Quote forms can be ordered inexpensively at OfficeDepot.com, Staples.com, OfficeMax.com.

STEP 79

Post Inventory Check List - Create the document you and your client will sign at the end of the Home Inventory process. This form is used to protect both you and the client. Include all disclaimers including statements outlining that you did not damage client items, will not share client information, etc.

STEP 80

Design and order **introductory postcards** announcing your new Home Inventory business, what a 3rd party Home Inventory is, and how you can be contacted. Do not spend a lot of money or time on these because mailings do not have the response typically seen by postcard campaigns in other industries. VistaPrint.com offers several free or low cost, high quality post cards. Many insurance agents will allow you to place postcards in their office or to add to their new customer packets.

STEP 81

Consider paying for referrals by creating a **Referral Partner Contract**. Referral Partners are non-competitive professionals that provide complimentary products and services to your Home Inventory business and seek the same target clients as you. Many people offer $25 or $50 referral fees, but do those really offer a true incentive for someone to take focus from their business? Why not offer a referral program where you pay a percentage of the project referred to you? This is the best and fastest way to create an entire army of salesmen working for you, and the best part is that you don't pay the referral fee until the client pays you!

Notes:

STEP 82

Join a **networking group**. Do not begin networking until **<u>after</u>** your pricing and processes have been well defined and you are able to quickly and concisely communicate what you do and what qualifies you to do it. Very important note: if you cannot clearly explain why and what you do in a few brief sentences, you are **<u>not</u>** ready to attend a networking meeting. Use your elevator speech you created in step #44 and you will be fine.

STEP 83

Define and seek out your best **strategic partners**. A strategic partnership is when a company combines forces with another company that has assets or services that will help the other, but does not want to manage internally. For example, a moving company has the ability to inventory a client project, but most moving companies do not want to perform the inventory and would prefer to send inventory clients to a HIP, sometimes for a finder's fee.

STEP 84

Introduce yourself and your company to local **Police and Fire** Departments. Most law and fire enforcement officials are very excited to learn of local HIPs. Although they typically are not permitted to refer clients to outside entities, they are a great resource for community educational and awareness events and oftentimes ask local HIPs to accompany them. Many cities, counties, and school districts allow local companies to apply to become an entity-approved vendor. Each entity has differing approval requirements, but requirements are typically straightforward. Once approved, law and fire enforcement is more able to recommend your HIP services.

STEP 85

Design generic **brochures** describing your company, products, history, and qualifications. Over time, you will have various brochures and marketing pieces to use for specific situations, but for now, create a basic brochure that can be used in any situation. Make sure your contact information is easily

Notes:

found. Have an experienced proofreader check and double check your work for typos, consistency, and flow. Use your style guide for faster designing and update as appropriate. Try to use unique photos; not the same five Microsoft photos found on nearly every other HIPs website.

STEP 86

With brochures in hand, **stop** at every insurance office you see while driving and introduce yourself and your products. When you begin this step, schedule one day per week to visit offices. Except for the price of gasoline, this is a free and very smart way to get face to face with your best referral partners!

STEP 87

Register to give free **community education classes** teaching residents how to perform their own home inventory. HOAs, Senior Centers, and neighborhood watch clubs are a good place to start. It may seem counter intuitive to teach people how inventory for themselves, but the truth is, once people realize that they need a Home Inventory, along with everything involved in the process, they are usually **more** than happy to have someone else do it for them. By doing this, you have also ensured that more people will be talking about you and your Home Inventory service. When you educate people, clients will find you!

STEP 88

Have and advertise a **Home Inventory Introductory Sale**. For example, $.25 per square foot instead of $.50 per square foot. Make sure you notify all networking connections, Insurance agents you just introduced yourself to, your seminar attendees, along with the law and fire enforcement agencies you have connected to. Don't forget to issue a press release announcing your sale and post relevant information on your website, Facebook Fan page, and Twitter stream.

Notes:

STEP 89

Perform your first formal **quote**. You have performed several 'practice' Home Inventories, spread the word about your products and services, and created a quote form. It is now time to perform a real quote for a stranger. Explain to your referral partners, Insurance agents, and your new networking acquaintances that you need experience giving quotes. Right now, do not worry about making a sale, your only objective is to get solid quote experience. Remember to send a thank you note and ask for feedback after the quote.

STEP 90

Connect with local connectors. This is another key step! Local connectors are easy to spot, they are the local business owners and decision makers that seem to be connected to everyone, attend key business events, and have their 'finger on the pulse' of the business community. Local connectors are relatively easy to find them on Facebook, Twitter, meetup.com, local business journals, and public calendars. Remember to connect, **really** connect by joining or starting the conversation, helping out at events, and being genuine. Listen do not just hear!

STEP 91

Find local **vendor events**. Be picky...only spend money or time on events with proven track records and reputations. As a new business owner, you will be inundated with 'the next big thing' – remember: they can't all be the best even in the universe! If you cannot afford a booth at a vendor event, go as an attendee. Nearly every attendee and booth participant can use an inventory so take plenty of business cards AND collect as many cards as possible. You can use these after the event to schedule follow up meetings and one-on-ones. Wear a polo shirt with your company logo.

STEP 92

Search **local activities** like National Night Out, festivals, etc. Make your presence known. Sponsor events and donate door prizes or silent auction items.

Notes:

Regarding donations: do not donate an entire Home Inventory. Instead, donate a portion or specific square footage. For example donate 1,000 square feet inventoried on a full project. Before donating anything, ensure that donators will receive free publicity such as listings in the newspaper or event program. Wear a polo shirt with your company logo.

STEP 93

Set a **social media schedule** including daily and weekly Tweets, blog posts, and Facebook entries. Most social media sites and tools are free, but they are invaluable in helping spread the word about you and your Home Inventory service. Consistency will go a long way toward establishing an on line presence. A strong on-line presence creates a buzz and solidifies your credibility and off-line reputation.

STEP 94

Create an aggressive **schedule to research** and communicate with potential referral and strategic partners. Outline type of partner, their industry, and what you can do for them. Set a goal for the number of contacts you want to make each week and stick to it. Track your progress – this will help get through the slower weeks when your Home Inventory service is still new.

STEP 95

Create an **annual press release schedule** outlining press releases. Although press releases are not as powerful as they once were, they are a valuable tool for giving you consistency and an on-line historical record of your Home Inventory service's activities. When completing your press release schedule, list dates and topic of press release. Setting up this schedule may take a bit, but the time spent setting this up will prove invaluable throughout the year. When looking for press release topics, consider holidays, local events, and important dates such as National Home Inventory Awareness Month in May. Educational advancements and industry conference attendance are reasons other good reasons to submit press releases.

Notes:

STEP 96

Define **one thing per month** on which to focus your advertising, social media, promotions, and special pricing. For example, some silly ideas include:

January: Updating Home Inventories to include new holiday gifts

February: Falling back in love with your homeowners insurance policy

March: Spring showers bring tornados and surges in power

April: Spring cleaning means time to update Home Inventory

May: National Home Inventory Awareness Month

June: Weddings and births time to update Home Inventory
July: Vacation time Home Inventories before going away

August: Back to School

September: Dorm room Home Inventories

October: Life without a current home inventory is frightening

November: Being thankful for taking inventory of holiday decorations

December: Taking inventory

STEP 97

Join or start a **Master Mind Group**. The Master Mind Group principle was introduced by Napoleon Hill in the early 1900s, but everyone who participates in Master Mind Groups agrees that they are one of the best ways to bring new and fresh ideas into your business. The Master Mind Group principle is based in the idea of being surrounded by a high-thinking support group to propel member to achieve success, both professionally and personally. I have participated in Master Mind Groups for several years and am still amazed at

Notes:

the incredible leaps and bounds each new Master Mind Group fosters. If you would like more information on Master Mind Groups, please email me at Michelle@ProveItsYours.com and I will be happy to send the guidelines and rules that have worked very well.

STEP 98

Flow your entire Home Inventory **process** and look for holes or duplicate steps in your process. If you do not know where to begin, Google Documents and Power Point have several free flow chart templates. If done attractively, your flow chart can also be a powerful marketing tool incorporated into your brochure. If you need help creating your flow chart, you can find many flow chart how-to articles and guides on line.

STEP 99

Volunteer at Rotary Clubs, Chambers of Commerce, Senior Centers, Lion's Clubs, etc. to educate how to perform Home Inventory. Now that you know your **entire** process, are comfortable explaining it, and have become an even better speaker with the help of Toast Masters, you are ready to give formal presentations. Most organizations will welcome an experienced speaking with a relevant topic that is willing to speak for free. Make sure you are ready and have a specific discount for these attendees. By now you know to wear your embroidered polo shirt.

STEP 100

Keep your camera handy for pictures on the road - always keep an eye out for possible photos supporting the need for Home Inventory including house fires, car accidents, police cars, areas sectioned off with 'Caution' tape, etc.

WHAT'S NEXT? After reviewing these ***First 100 Steps to HIP Success***, you feel necessary steps are missing, please email me at Michelle@ProveItsYours.com. If the step you submit is added to this list, you will be mailed a printed book in the newest version.

ABOUT MICHELLE KETTERMAN

Being the victim of a devastating home robbery in 1996, Michelle Ketterman understands first hand how difficult recalling everything you own can be during an emotional and stressful event; only to be compounded while dealing with the emotional toll the robbery took on her children, spouse, and herself.

After the robbery, Michelle and her husband learned the expensive lesson that without a current home inventory, you can literally be victimized twice: once by the event, and then sadly by your own lack of preparedness by not having a complete list of what you own.

Although the Kettermans had excellent Home Owners Insurance and would have been reimbursed for everything, the emotional aftermath of the robbery caused them to inadvertently leave many valuable and rarely used items from the claim reimbursement form.

Learning this expensive and painful lesson propelled Michelle to start keeping detailed documentation and photographs of everything in the Ketterman home. After seeing the detailed lists Michelle kept of her belongings, and becoming discouraged by the amount of time and effort it took, friends and family asked Michelle to compile the same lists for them. Word began to spread that what others weren't able to do after months of work, Michelle easily completed home inventories after spending just a few hours in their home.

In the past 15 years, Michelle has honed her craft and enjoys educating home and business owners of the importance of keeping a third party home inventory. She takes great pride in providing an honest and well-needed service at a reasonable price, and thoroughly enjoys meeting other small business owners and sharing ideas.

After learning that many Home Inventory Professionals falsely claim they are licensed when there is no license in the Home Inventory industry, Michelle gathered passionate peers from around the country dedicated to consumer education and ethical professional standards, and formed The Inventory

Institute. A national organization that verifies Home Inventory Professionals and their insurance, bonding, and inventory practices; The Inventory Institute is the first of its kind and is propelling the industry forward ethically.

Michelle, along with Advisory Board members of The Inventory Institute scheduled and coordinated the first ever Home Inventory Professional's annual conference. The conference helped ring in a new era of open communication and camaraderie for Home Inventory Professionals. As technology increases, so do questionable and suspicious Home Inventory products and services -- Michelle and members of The Inventory Institute are fiercely committed to protect and educate property owners and ethical Home Inventory Professionals.

Michelle wrote and launched the nation's first professional certification program and has written many industry resources and has recorded many training DVDs and programs.

Michelle is an active community member and passionately supports Toast Masters and various local business and networking organizations.

Michelle has 20 years experience in database design and maintenance, process and procedures manual writing, credentialing, and event planning.

WHERE TO FIND MICHELLE:

On Facebook at:
Facebook.com/TheInventoryInstitute and Facebook.com/TheInventoryExperts and Facebook.com/MichelleKettermanTheInventoryExpert

On Twitter at: @ExpertInventory and @Inventory_News

On-line at: TheInventoryInstitute.com, ProveItsYours.com, and LearnInventory.com

MORE HIP RESOURCES

Digital books found on Amazon.com:

"The Home Inventory Profession; How to be an Expert" by Michelle Ketterman

"The Authoritative Home Inventory Professional Lists - Books 1-7" by Michelle Ketterman and Patrick Martin

CLASSES:
LearnInventory.com

INDUSTRY INFORMATION:
TheInventoryInstitute.com

GREAT FREE RESOURCES:
VistaPrint.com, Zoho.com, MailChimp.com

20543399R00044

Made in the USA
Lexington, KY
08 February 2013